AU

With more than 1.5 million books sold to date, Adam Croft is one of the most successful independently published authors in the world, and one of the biggest selling authors of the past few years.

His 2015 worldwide bestseller *Her Last Tomorrow* sold more than 200,000 copies across all platforms and became one of the bestselling books of the year, reaching the top 10 in the overall Amazon Kindle chart and peaking at number 12 in the combined paperback fiction and non-fiction chart.

His *Knight & Culverhouse* crime thriller series has sold more than 250,000 copies worldwide, with his *Kempston Hardwick* mystery books being adapted as audio plays starring some of the biggest names in British TV.

In 2016, the *Knight & Culverhouse Box Set* reached storewide number 1 in Canada, knocking J.K. Rowling's *Harry Potter and the Cursed Child* off the top spot only weeks after *Her Last Tomorrow* was also number 1 in Canada. The new edition of *Her Last*

*Tomorrow* also reached storewide number 1 in Australia over Christmas 2016.

During the summer of 2016, two of Adam's books hit the *USA Today* bestseller list only weeks apart, making them two of the most-purchased books in the United States over the summer.

In February 2017, *Only The Truth* became a worldwide bestseller, reaching storewide number 1 at both Amazon US and Amazon UK, making it the bestselling book in the world at that moment in time. The same day, Amazon's overall Author Rankings placed Adam as the most widely read author in the world, with J.K. Rowling in second place.

In January 2018, Adam's bestselling book to date, *Tell Me I'm Wrong* became a worldwide bestseller and has since gone on to sell more than 250,000 copies.

Adam has been featured on BBC television, *BBC Radio 4*, *BBC Radio 5 Live*, the *BBC World Service*, *The Guardian*, *The Huffington Post*, *The Bookseller* and a number of other news and media outlets.

In March 2018, Adam was conferred as an Honorary Doctor of Arts, the highest academic qualification in the UK, by the University of Bedfordshire in recognition of his achievements.

Adam presents the regular crime fiction podcast

*Partners in Crime* with fellow bestselling author Robert Daws.

facebook.com/IndieAuthorMindset

twitter.com/adamcroft

instagram.com/adamcroftbooks

# INTRODUCTION

The importance of blurbs and hooks cannot be overstated. But I'm going to try anyway.

It would be fair to say that discovering the importance of blurbs and hooks — and unlocking how to write a good one — quite literally changed my life.

Before December 2015 I'd never given blurbs a second thought. They were a necessary evil, a part of the publishing process which couldn't be avoided.

Like many authors, I presumed the blurb was meant to be a quick précis of the book's plot and characters, to let the reader know what the story's about.

I couldn't have been more wrong. And I found out in dramatic style.

I'll make no bones about it — I discovered how to

write a killer blurb and hook entirely by accident. My entire career has been far less the product of any sort of genius and much more a series of happy accidents which I've later deconstructed and recreated. But I have deconstructed it, and I have recreated it. Numerous times.

I'll be honest, I've also failed numerous times. You will too. There is no magic bullet in publishing, and no surefire way to *make* people buy any book. All we can do is increase the odds of them doing so, and forming a killer blurb or hook is one of the quickest, easiest — and certainly cheapest — ways of increasing those odds big time.

There are lots of different pieces of conflicting information out there when it comes to blurbs. The advice I'll give in this book conflicts quite a lot with what's already out there. But I have two responses to that.

First, my advice comes from two places. Not only have I been there and done it and had huge success through using killer blurbs and hooks, but I've come at it from a different angle — psychology. I'm a keen student of psychology and have been for almost twenty years, when I first studied it academically. The psychology of persuasion is a particularly favourite subject of mine. This is the basis of my method for writing killer blurbs and hooks.

Second, it's fair to say that it's difficult — if not

almost impossible — to stand out from the vast and ever-increasing crowd in the modern publishing industry. More often than not, just being *different* can go a long way to helping you stand out. And my method is different.

I don't go in for the hard sell. I reject the notion that a call to action is a necessary part of a book description. I don't conform to convention in respect of blurbs, in much the same way I don't in any other part of my career or life. And that's not entirely innate or accidental.

There are a lot of aspects and influences which have gone into my method of writing blurbs and hooks. (Feel free to call it the Croft Method. That sort of thing is *super* marketable, not to mention great for my ego.) In this book, I'm going to talk you through them and give you all the background you need to write your own.

I should also mention that this book is designed to accompany my online mini-course, also cunningly titled *Writing Killer Blurbs and Hooks.* You can find it at https://courses.indieauthormindset.com. As a thank you for buying this book, I'll even give you an extra 40% off the course when you enter the coupon code EBOOK40 at the checkout. There are unique tips and aspects in both the course and the book, so I and my bank manager heartily recommend buying both.

If you've already taken the course and paid full

price, fear not. The EBOOK40 discount can be used on ANY of my courses, current and future, at https:// courses.indieauthormindset.com. It's yours for life as a thank you for buying this book.

# PART 1
# BLURBS

# WHY ARE BLURBS SO IMPORTANT?

The publishing industry has changed on an unrecognisable scale over the last decade. Readers no longer buy books primarily from bookstores. With that, certain signals which attract readers to books are no longer relevant, whilst others have become more relevant.

Generally speaking, there are four things readers look at when they're deciding whether or not to buy a book. Based on my own research, plus reading that of others, speaking to some big-name authors and adding a large splash of anecdotal evidence, it's generally agreed that these are the four most important aspects:

1. Cover
2. Blurb/product description
3. Price

4. Reviews

That's also accepted by most people to be the order of importance.

Of course, there are many other aspects at play here. For example, your book's congruence with what the reader is looking for is probably the highest, but that's not a physical aspect or anything you can change.

In terms of what authors have control over, these are the four most important things a reader takes into account when deciding whether or not to buy your book.

Why is the cover the most important? Quite simply, it's the first thing they see. I have a little saying: **Never judge a book by its cover, unless it's a book.**

Potential readers will usually see your book's cover *before* even getting to your product page. They'll likely see it in thumbnail form in a search results page, Amazon ad or some other form of marketing. True enough, on at least two of those feeding points the reader will also see your price and overall review score, but those two elements actually fall much further down the list at this stage and only come into play when balanced against everything else on your product page. Most crucially, that's your blurb.

Readers will happily pay top dollar for a book they

really want. Likewise, they'll not bother to shell out a measly 99 cents on a book which doesn't appeal. Most won't even download a freebie if it doesn't sound like they'll enjoy it. Why would they? There are a ton of books out there.

Let's have a look at each of those four factors in turn.

## 1. Cover

Although this is generally accepted to be the most important aspect when it comes to selling your book, there's not a huge difference between this and the next most important aspect.

It's also very expensive and time consuming to get a new cover designed. If you're hiring the sort of designer who's going to make a real difference, you're looking at a few hundred dollars and a waiting list of anything up to six months.

## 3. Price

The more astute amongst you will have noticed I've skipped straight to point 3. That's deliberate. You're an author. You get dramatic effect, right?

Pricing can be updated with relative ease, but will also have a large impact on your bottom line. If you drop your price from \$2.99 to \$1.99, for example, you also drop your royalty rate from 70% to 35% on Amazon, without even taking into account that the lower retail price will reduce your royalty further.

In fact, your royalty will drop from just over \$2 to under 70 cents. You'd need to guarantee selling at least three times as many books — just from that slight price drop — to make it worthwhile considering.

Price drops — and increases — do definitely affect sales levels. But I'm yet to see anyone's sales triple by shaving a dollar off the price. I'd far sooner recommend making your book more appealing and potentially even raising the price as a result of increased demand.

## 4. Reviews

Authors obsess over reviews, and I've never been sure why. I rarely even ask readers to leave reviews any more, as I've seen no major difference in the marketability of a book with hundreds (or thousands) of reviews and those with few or none.

Sure, there is a difference, but it's so small compared to the swings that can be achieved elsewhere that it's relatively insignificant. Reviews follow sales. The reverse is not necessarily true.

Spend some time on any readers' forum or group on

Facebook and you'll see far more powerful forces at play than reviews on a product page. Sure, they're important to some, but most readers will tell you they don't pay any real attention to reviews other than the overall product score. And that only requires one review.

What's more, you've no real way to influence reviews or control who posts them, so why waste your time worrying about them?

## 2. Blurb/product description

Ah, dramatic effect, my old friend. It's good to see you back.

Compared to having your cover redesigned, updating your blurb is completely free, not to mention much easier and less time consuming.

Compared to changing your price, it carries relatively little risk of slicing your income by two thirds or making your book look cheap.

And compared to worrying about reviews, your blurb is something you can actually change — and which actually matters.

This is the one place where you get complete creative control. And it can make a huge difference.

## Putting it in perspective

For a writer, I quite like numbers. They don't like me back, but that's not the point.

Let's assume that by tweaking your blurbs across your whole backlist, you manage to sell just one extra book a day. Not one extra copy of each of your books — one book total. Your entire daily sales increase by just one copy. Now, I'm guessing that sounds both disappointing and achievable, yes?

It's actually only one of those.

If your book is priced at $3.99, that one extra sale a day amounts to $84 a month, or $1,000 across a year. If you keep your books on sale for the next ten years (and why wouldn't you?) that small, free edit to your blurb will have earned you $10,000. Not bad for an hour's work, eh? And that is quite literally the lowest possible daily increase you could see. Just one extra sale a day.

What difference could that extra $1,000 a year make to you? It's a free holiday, a couple of mortgage payments or a lot of beer. Please don't make me choose.

All joking aside (and I'm not joking — I'd totally choose the beer) spending an hour or so reworking your blurb could completely revolutionise your book sales.

So yeah. Kinda important.

## WHY MOST AUTHORS GET BLURBS WRONG

Let me get one thing straight from the start. **A blurb and a synopsis are not the same thing.**

Many writers know this, but still don't understand the importance of it and will craft blurbs which are a cut-down version of the synopsis with the ending snipped off and a mysterious 'who knows what'll happen' closer added, complete with even more mysterious ellipses...

Please don't do this. *This* is what most authors get wrong with their blurbs. And no you can't skip to the next chapter. I've got more complaining to do.

Your blurb is your book's sales pitch. It is designed to **sell** the book. It is not designed to tell readers what happens in the book. That's what, y'know, the book is for.

All your blurb should do is convince readers to pick the book up. Sounds simple, right? On the face of it, it is. But the methods and techniques for actually achieving that are where the difficulties tend to come in.

At its root, this is all about psychology. There are a number of different blurb-writing methods and services out there, and most of them have their merits.

In general, though, they tend to be a little top-down in their approach. They're based on trying different things and seeing what works for the majority of people. They're based on rather formulaic strategies.

Now, formulaic strategies aren't a bad thing. If there's a winning formula, there's a winning formula. But that approach neglects one important fact: Not everybody can win.

The more people in the field who apply the 'winning formula', the higher the number of people applying that formula who won't actually win. At this point, can it be considered a winning formula?

The people who have the most success with any given technique in any given field are the pioneers, closely followed by the early adopters, then barely followed at all by the bandwagoners and sheep.

Think of Dick Fosbury. Go on. Just for a little bit. You what? Oh, right. I'd better explain then.

Dick Fosbury was an American high jumper. Still is, in fact. American, I mean. I doubt he's still a high jumper at his age, although he might be. You never know. Unless he dies between me writing this and you reading it, I mean.

Before Dick came along, every high jumper in history had their own particular way of getting over the bar. Some ran hell for leather at the jumpy thing, then jumped up in the air and threw themselves forward over the bar like a fat bloke learning to dive for the first time. Others straddled it like a massive hurdle. Some even rolled over the bar like they were falling out of bed. Madness, I know.

Dick Fosbury decided to try something different. He ran at the big bar thing at a rather bizarre angle, then at the last minute he turned his body so he went over the bar *backwards*, arching his back as he did so. He looked like an absolute nutter. But he won every single high jump competition he entered.

The authorities tried telling him he wasn't jumping in the proper way, but there was no rule that said you had to run in a straight line and belly flop over the bar, so Dick carried on with what became known as the Fosbury Flop, winning every competition in sight.

Sooner or later, the other competitors decided enough was enough, and they started Fosbury Flopping like there was no tomorrow. All of a sudden, the gap between Dick and the others began to shrink. The Fosbury Flop was now *de rigeur*, and anyone trying to do the high jump in the old, traditional manner would be laughed off the athletics field in the same way I was when I ran the 400m in middle school and Chris Bearton tripped me up and made me land flat on my face, the bastard. Not that I'm bitter.

My point is that the Fosbury Flop no longer stands out. Just turning up and doing the Fosbury Flop no longer guarantees victory. In fact, statistically speaking, the vast majority of high jumpers doing the Fosbury Flop *won't* win any given competition.

Unfortunately, no-one has yet discovered a more successful way of launching one's body over a metal pole, so my analogy falls tantalisingly short of the finish line, just like I did when Chris bloody Bearton tripped me up.

Following the formula only works for a short period of time. After that, a new formula needs to be invented or discovered.

But why has the Fosbury Flop never been bettered? Presumably because there is no better way of jumping over a pole. Sports scientists will, no doubt, have done computer modelling and simulations to try and discover a better method, but failed.

Science and biology has shown them that by working upwards from the rudimentary facts and unchangeable biological basics (running in a curved line means you can lower your centre of gravity, spines are quite bendy) they could find *their* perfect way of getting people over the bar.

That's why working upwards, in a bottom-up approach, from the basic, known psychological facts and aspects of human behaviour which never change, you can use those principles and apply them to your own books and create your own killer blurbs and hooks.

There are no recipes. There's no secret sauce. But I'm going to give you all the best ingredients and a few tips on method in order to ensure you can create a flavour which tastes perfect for your specific audience.

Now, I can't promise I won't use any more silly analogies, but I'm definitely done with high jumps and sauce. Let's move on.

# WHAT MAKES A GOOD BLURB?

As anyone who writes, reads or explore across multiple genres will know, different things work for different readers in different genres.

A thriller blurb will look very different from a literary fiction or romance blurb. But my advice and method isn't so much about the content or the wording itself, but the structure of your blurb and the relationship between blurb and reader, as well as blurb and book.

## Hit the right tone

Many authors have a tendency to write dry, uninspiring blurbs because they're in synopsis mode rather than selling mode.

Give your potential readers a flavour of the tone they're going to get in the book itself. Give them a feel for the style.

Writing a thriller? Your blurb will be short. Snappy. To the point. The words will be explosive. The atmosphere will be high-octane. And the stakes? High.

If your book is literary fiction, for example, you'll be looking at longer, flowing sentences which give the reader an insight into the style of the work itself. It's what those readers have come to expect, after all, and it would be a crying shame to disappoint.

With romance, you'll want to communicate the passion. Emotions and feelings will be running high. Everything is at stake. Families could be torn apart, and characters are forced to alter their perspectives for love.

## Keep the gold above the fold

You don't have long to hook a reader. Many authors will end their blurb on a cliffhanger or put their strongest stuff at the end, so the reader is desperate to buy by the time they get to that point. But there's one huge problem with that.

Most readers *won't* get to that point. Why? Go and look at a book on Amazon, Apple Books, Kobo or any of the other major retailers. You'll see that only a small portion of the start of the blurb shows, with the reader having to click to view the rest.

**Amazon Kindle**

**Apple Books**

**Barnes & Noble NOOK**

As you can see, each retailer has its own cut-off point at which the reader will have to click to read more of the blurb. By that point, the reader needs to have been hooked either into wanting to read more or, even better, into buying the book.

It's wise to ensure your blurbs are tweaked to suit

each retailer, ensuring you keep the gold above the fold and ensure your strongest material is visible to everyone who hits the sales page and not just those who choose to read more of your blurb.

## Take out all unnecessary words

Keep your blurb brief. We're used to having 100,000 words in which to get a message across, but your blurb requires the exact opposite mindset.

You need to convince someone to pick your book up in as few words as possible. With *Her Last Tomorrow*, that was done with just nine words. Of course, that was actually too short for most retailers to allow as a blurb so I had to add a more conventional blurb under that main tagline, where the real challenge became trying not to dilute that strong hook.

Read through your blurb and judge each word on its own merits. Yes. Each word. If there's a better, stronger, more active word, use it. If the sentence works just as well — or better — without that word, remove it. Keep your blurb lean and ensure that every single word pulls its own weight.

## Keep them moving

The reason for the austerity of words mentioned a moment ago is that readers' attention spans are very short online. The internet is designed to ensure people can get what they want easily and quickly.

On any given Amazon product page, for example, there'll be anything from twenty up to one hundred other books being advertised. Even at a direct mathematical average, that gives you a 1-5% chance of converting the reader to buy your book.

You might assume a reader will read your whole blurb. They won't. Online attention spans are far, far shorter than any reasonable person might imagine, which is why every word needs to pull its own weight. It's also why you need to keep the reader moving.

Each line, each paragraph needs to end in a way which pulls the reader on to the next line. They can't possibly *not* read on. And how do you do that?

Like that, for example. That paragraph ended on a question, which is just one technique which compels you to read on to find out the answer. And there's a powerful reason for that.

It's psychology. It's the same thing that made you read on from *that* paragraph, too. You understood I was about to tell you the powerful reason, but you'd have to read on to find it out. I didn't *tell* you that, but your brain inferred it from the wording I used.

## Make the desire theirs

In terms of the psychology of persuasion, most people will trust their own instincts and thought processes, then the advice of close friends and family, then the advice or instructions of a complete stranger. To potential readers, you fall into the last category.

That's why recommendations and direct word-of-mouth are considered to be the most powerful forms of marketing. And they are super powerful. But they're not the *most* powerful. Take a look at that hierarchy again.

1. Own instincts and thought processes
2. Advice of close family and friends
3. Advice or instructions of a complete stranger

Even more powerful than recommendations and direct word-of-mouth are decisions or impulses made in the reader's brain. Let's go back to the hook for *Her Last Tomorrow*.

*Could you murder your wife to save your daughter?*

The reason that worked so well is it made the reader *want* to buy the book. It fired off a reaction in their brain which made them *have* to buy the book.

Not once did I say 'You'll love this book!' or 'Buy this great book now!'. That just comes across as sales-like. Of course you want them to buy the book. You're selling it. You would say that. But if the desire comes from the buyer themselves, that's extraordinarily powerful.

Take a look at Apple. They're one of the biggest companies to ever exist. They were the first trillion-dollar organisation on the planet. But they very rarely advertise and when they do they're not pushy. Instead, they extol the virtues of their products. They sell a dream. They show you how great your life will be with the latest iPhone or horrendously-priced set of ear buds. And you *want* them. No-one from Apple calls you up or suggests you might want to buy it. You go flocking to them because they've managed to make you think that desire has come from within you. And whaddya know? They're ready and waiting to sell to you.

# TROPES

My dictionary defines a trope as 'a significant or recurring theme; a motif'.

Tropes are everywhere in fiction, from characters to covers. Think of the motif of a knife dripping with blood, and you immediately think of crime fiction. See a character called Knaarsgard the Viking and you've got a fair idea of which genre(s) that book might be. Read a blurb with the words 'hunky', 'reverse harem' and 'steamy encounters' and you're probably looking at some pretty heavy romance, verging on erotica.

This is, largely, all about branding. When you look at a book's cover you know exactly what you're getting. The imagery, typography and even the title itself will (or at least should) tell you exactly what you're letting yourself in for.

It's a psychological shortcut which stops us reading the blurb of every single book in the shop or — worse — reading every book in the shop, before we get to find out which ones we like and don't like.

In short, it's a filtering system which enables our brains to make quick, snap decisions. We'll be looking at that in a lot more detail in the *Understanding the psychology* section of this book. Whatever you do, don't skip that section. It's probably the most important part and underpins the whole system I use to write killer blurbs and hooks. It's also something which I don't think has been properly explored or addressed elsewhere.

Tropes are a good thing when it comes to our industry. It means we crime writers don't have to deal with romance readers wondering where the steamy sex scenes have gone, or military sci-fi fans wanting to know why there were no spaceships. It allows people who want to read our sort of book to find it quickly and easily.

When it comes to blurbs, tropes need careful management. Making it clear your book is a crime thriller is one thing, but ending every blurb with 'Can the detective find the killer before it's too late...?' is neither original nor compelling. As with sci-fi, a deadly disease which threatens to wipe out all of humanity is nothing we haven't seen before. Yes, both tropes leave us in absolutely no doubt as to which genres the books are in, but they also lack originality and aren't going to stand out in any way.

There's no secret formula for the balancing act between putting out recognisable tropes and remaining original. It's one of those times when the proof is in the pudding. Fortunately, changing the wording in your blurb can be done very quickly and easily as an indie author, so even if you get it wrong it's far from being the end of the world.

As far as tropes go, in this book we're looking specifically at blurbs, so I trawled the bestseller lists on Amazon at the time of writing this book and noted down a few tropes and words which crop up time and time again in the blurbs of the bestsellers.

## Crime

- dead
- investigate
- suspicion
- murdered
- discovers
- killer
- dangerous
- secrets

## Epic fantasy

- empire
- strangers
- fortune
- honour
- enemy
- revenge
- betrayal
- fate
- magic

## Western

- Governor
- saloon
- family
- war
- brothers
- ranch
- soldier
- Indians
- rustlers
- outlaws

Erotica

- sex
- passion
- lust
- fantasy
- desire
- love
- souls
- seduction
- curiosity
- dominance

Military sci-fi

- planets
- interplanetary
- resources
- empire
- war
- humanity
- mission
- alien
- technology

- weapons
- space
- enemy
- victory

Let's face it: if you found a blurb with the words 'lust', 'seduction' and 'dominance' in, you'd have a fair idea of the genre of the book. The same goes for 'magic', 'honour' and 'empire'. Likewise 'murdered', 'investigate' and 'killer'.

These are all tropes and trigger words which clearly elucidate the subject matter of the book. Nowhere does it say 'this is a crime fiction book' or 'this is an epic fantasy novel'. That is all spoken through the choice of words in the blurb itself.

When you're writing your blurb, consider the tropes and trigger words for your specific genre and how you can use them in your blurb or advertising copy.

Speaking of which...

# CONVERTING YOUR BLURB FOR ADVERTISING

Your blurb, as we've already covered, *is* advertising copy. That's precisely its purpose on your sales page: to convince a potential reader to buy the book.

When most authors talk of advertising copy, though, they're usually referring to the small amount of text Amazon Advertising (formerly AMS, and probably under yet another name by the time you read this) lets you insert into certain on-site ads, or the copy used in a Facebook advert.

And that's all fair enough. After all, even the leanest and most concise blurb is going to be too long for most Facebook ads and will definitely blow the character limit over at Amazon Advertising.

So how do you condense your blurb down into

usable sales copy for these advertising platforms? And what actually *works*?

I should add a caveat at this point in time. This book, like all of the advice I give under my Indie Author Mindset brand, is designed to be evergreen. It won't (or shouldn't) date. For that reason, I'm not going to go into the specific character limit that Amazon Advertising has at the time of writing, as it'll probably have changed by the time I go to print. I'm not going to go into what specific styles of sales copy work right now either, because the overwhelming likelihood is they won't be as effective six months down the line.

There are industry gurus — and plenty of them — who specialise in being on the ball with all the latest trends and hot new things. That's not me. I couldn't stand the stress of keeping up with it all. What I *am* going to do, though, is distill down exactly what makes readers want to click your ad or buy your book at an ad copy level, before they even get to your product page.

It's worth considering your product page as being the final step that convinces potential readers to buy your book. Nothing should come as a surprise at this point, at least not a nasty surprise. Is your book priced at five or six bucks? Slip that in somewhere before they get to the sales page and feel as though they've been victim to a bait and switch. Is the book free or 99 cents? That's a nice surprise, but is an even more marketable selling point which can — and should — be used in your advertising copy.

At the time of writing, Amazon Advertising displays most ads in such a way that the price is always visible, so no worries there. That piece of advice mainly pertains to Facebook and BookBub Ads, as well as any new platforms which pop up after the genesis of this particular book.

So what elements do you need to consider?

## Hammer home the genre

This is all about connecting the product with the reader, and there are a number of ways of letting them know this is the sort of book they'd like.

Quotes from reviews can often be useful here. *'The best epic fantasy series for years!' 'Superb high-octane thrillers.' 'A heart-wrenching love story.'* All of those — if real quotes — accurately convey the style and genre of the book at the same time as providing social proof from a reviewer or reader.

Take note of that little method. Managing to merge two psychological sales tactics in one element is gold dust when you're trying to shoehorn everything into a limited number of words, characters or screen space.

## Convey the pull

Generally speaking, this is about stakes. Most genre fiction has some element of stakes which the main character has to overcome. In thrillers, it'll be the impossible choice or some form of impending doom. In romance it'll be the will-they-won't-they. In general, it's the bit that conveys 'How the hell are they going to sort this shit out?'

Again, you need to stand out. Every thriller conveys some sort of impending doom which only one person can avoid. Every military sci-fi novel threatens the end of civilisation. Every romance novel carries the risk of broken love and heartbreak. What makes yours different? How can you convey that pull without sounding trite and clichéd?

## Be succinct

The key is to get everything across in as few words as possible. This isn't a new concept: it's something advertisers have had to do for years. Movie producers have come up with simple but effective loglines for years. And it works.

The most succinct way of getting your book's tone, genre, content, pull and audience across is with a really killer hook.

On which note...

# PART 2
# HOOKS

# A NOTE ABOUT HOOKS

Hooks aren't strictly necessary, but they can make a huge difference to your book if you get them right.

They're similar in form to an elevator pitch or movie tagline. You're trying to hook people in with very few words, each designed to have maximum dramatic impact.

I've done this a couple of times with my psychological thrillers, the two biggest selling of which have been *Tell Me I'm Wrong* and *Her Last Tomorrow*.

The hook — or elevator pitch — for *Her Last Tomorrow* is:

**Could you murder your wife to save your daughter?**

Let's break that down bit by bit and see why it's so effective.

First of all, the book is a domestic psychological thriller. It's told from the viewpoint of the parents whose daughter is kidnapped. That is every parent's worst nightmare. Primal fears triggered — check.

But it gets better than that. Look at the pronouns.

Could **you** murder **your** wife to save **your** daughter?

Not *Could Nick Connor murder his wife to save his daughter?* No-one reading the blurb knows who Nick is, nor do they care about his life. But make it about *your reader* and you've got an extremely powerful hook within this genre.

Domestic psychological thrillers are designed to feel personal, as if you could be the protagonist. They allow you to follow the characters' thoughts and feelings as they go through dreadful situations.

Note also that it's not asking *will* Nick or you murder his/your wife to save his/your daughter, but *could* you. It's a question that needs answering, which calls your primal self into action and tugs at every human emotion.

On a psychological level, all questions need answering. When we see one, we feel the need to either answer it ourselves or somehow determine what the answer could be. When it's a question as powerful as this, that effect is multiplied many times.

It also has an element of choice. For most parents, that choice would be an obvious one, but it's still there. The more difficult you can make that choice, the better. Think of *Sophie's Choice*, in which the main character has to decide which of her children lives.

Likewise, when I released *Tell Me I'm Wrong* in 2018, I used this hook:

**What if you discovered your husband was a serial killer?**

Again, a direct question. It needs answering.

What if **you** discovered **your** husband was a serial killer? It's personalised. It puts the reader in the mind of the protagonist — something that's common, if not essential to the psychological thriller genre.

It's domestic. It's normal. Until the last two words turn everything on its head and leave the reader gasping.

That book outsold *Her Last Tomorrow* almost immediately, showing that the power of a great hook is not only still there, but it's growing.

As always, standing out from the crowd is the key. Don't look at what other people do and try to copy it. You wouldn't win many races if you ran ten feet behind the guy in front, copying his every move. You'd never win and you'd look pretty daft.

Lots of authors have tried to do this. I've lost count of the number of *Her Last* books I've seen released since 2015. I can't even tell you how many slightly-tweaked hooks of mine I've seen being used. I've even had major publishers blatantly ripping off my titles, covers and plots. But none of them have succeeded. And that's because they did the complete opposite of standing out and being original.

This wasn't meant to be a chapter on originality and standing out in a crowded market, but there's no denying that is the deeper purpose of a hook from a marketing point of view.

And the simple fact of the matter is that this is exactly where you, as an indie author, can take the bull by the horns and gain a massive advantage, because even the big publishers do this really, really badly.

For example, when a publisher took on the rights to *Her Last Tomorrow* and republished it as a new edition, they wrote a new blurb which I thought was pretty drab and uninspiring. But that's not the worst bit. The blurb didn't even include the hook ('Could you murder your wife to save your daughter?'). It wasn't there. At all.

This was the hook that sold 150,000 copies of the book within a matter of weeks and which Thomas & Mercer admitted had drawn them towards me and made them want to acquire the rights to the book. They loved it. They thought it was revolutionary. Yet when they wrote their blurb, it wasn't there.

I gently pointed out that perhaps it might be an idea to include it *somewhere*, to which they replied to tell me yes, I was quite right, it would be better if the hook was there, front and centre. Why did I have to tell them this? I'm a guy sitting in his spare bedroom writing crime novels. These people are high-end publishers working for the biggest company ever to have existed on this planet.

So, to summarise, don't assume the successful authors and publishers are doing it right. 99% of the time their success is not linked to their blurb. Instead, it'll be linked to an enormous marketing budget and wider advertising campaign which can paper over the cracks on the sales page itself. As an indie author with a limited budget, you don't have the luxury of throwing money at the issue and hoping for the best. (As an aside, my spellcheck tried changing that to 'throwing Moet at the issue', which would be undeniably more original, not to mention delicious.)

Now that all that negativity is out of the way, let's have a look at what you *should* be doing if you want to write a killer blurb and hook for your book.

## WHAT MAKES A HOOK HOOKY?

On the whole, this is untrodden ground. There are a number of books and resources on book marketing and writing techniques, but the concept of distilling down that marketing hook for your book is something that's been pretty much ignored by most industry experts.

It's a subject which I'm very keen on, due to the success I've had through developing killer hooks for a couple of my own books.

Again, here are the two hooks which have been the most successful for me:


1. *Could you murder your wife to save your daughter?*

. . .

2. *What if you discovered your husband was a serial killer?*

Both those hooks include at least two ingredients of killer hooks, depending on how we're defining them.

Each of them poses a **question**. Questions stand out. They require an answer. The human brain is programmed to seek resolution at all costs. That's why minor chords always resolve to a nice round major in musical pieces (and sound disconcerting when they don't). It's why newspapers and websites use questions in their clickbait headlines to attract readers and advertising hits. If a question is posed, it needs answering. And, in each of my example hooks, the answer lies within the book.

Let's take the questions out and rephrase them as immediate sentences, and see what happens.

*Could you murder your wife to save your daughter?*
*You have to murder your wife to save your daughter.*

*What if you discovered your husband was a serial killer?*
*You discover your husband is a serial killer.*

. . .

Sure, they're still intriguing and enticing, but it's hard to ignore the fact that a huge part of the hook is lost.

(At this point, it's worth me also mentioning that humans *love* to share their opinions in response to leading questions. We can't help ourselves, despite the fact that everyone else cares about our opinions as much as we care about theirs. I've run a number of Facebook ads which asked readers to vote for their favourite between two detectives, and user engagement was always sky high.)

Both of the above hooks also make strong use of **personal pronouns**. Each of them uses a *you* and a *your*. Why? The reader isn't a character in either of those books.

Let's use the characters' names and see how the hooks sound.

*Could you murder your wife to save your daughter?*

*Can Nick Connor murder his wife to save his daughter?*

*What if you discovered your husband was a serial killer?*

*What if Megan Miller discovered her husband was a serial killer?*

Who gives a shit, right? Who's Nick Connor? And Megan Miller? Do you know either of these people? Nope. But you know *you*. You care about you. By putting *you* in those situations and asking how you'd react, you're instantly and irrevocably linked with the story.

The hook for *Her Last Tomorrow* also has an **impossible choice**. Nick either has to murder his wife or never see his daughter again. Neither of them are choices you'd want to take unless you're in a particularly unhappy marriage, so not only is it a question — and a personalised question at that — it's also one that can't easily be answered.

This, to some extent, goes for the *Tell Me I'm Wrong* hook, too. What the hell *would* you do if you discovered your husband was a serial killer? The moral responses to both questions might be obvious, but a huge number of people will be desperate to see how it plays out and how on earth a normal person could handle such a situation.

Read those words again. *'Desperate to see how it plays out and how on earth a normal person could handle such a situation.'* That is, in a nutshell, the essence of a psychological thriller. It is an unmistakeable **marker of genre**. Neither of those hooks scream sci-fi or young adult fantasy. It's clear from each of them what type of book this will be.

*Tell Me I'm Wrong* also makes good use of a **what if** scenario. I use *what if*s a <u>lot</u>. Most of my plots and storylines come from a *what if* moment. Try it now. Look around you. Perhaps you're reading this book on a train. *What if* the train derailed and crashed and you were the only survivor? There's a story for you, in a matter of seconds.

Maybe you're sitting at home reading this. *What if* a plane crashed outside? *What if* the doorbell went and it was someone you hadn't seen for twenty years and never wanted to see again?

The *what if* scenario can be played at any moment, anywhere. Let your imagination run away with you and see what you come up with. More likely than not, they are scenarios which can be developed as hooks. Why? Because they're situations in which normality is suddenly and unexpectedly disrupted — the incendiary device for most good stories and most killer hooks.

There are a number of other authors who 'get' hooks. One such author is Steve Cavanagh, a fellow British crime writer, who wrote what I believe is the best hook

I've ever seen. It sends shivers down my spine every time I see it, and has done it again as I anticipate typing the words here:

*The serial killer isn't on trial. He's on the jury.*

That's the hook for Steve's book *Thirteen*, and I think you'll agree it's an absolute stunner. This is the perfect example of the **twist of logic**. You're set up with something perfectly normal, then *BOOM*, it's ripped from you, twisted around and thrown back in your face.

*The serial killer isn't on trial.* Alright. That's quite normal. So what, he hasn't been caught yet? They arrested and tried the wrong person? Jeez, that's terrible, but I'm not exactly compelled to pick up the...

*He's on the jury.* BLOODY HELL. See what I mean? Smack. Straight in the face. The complete opposite of what you'd expect. The serial killer's on the *jury*? At the trial of his murders? Woah.

That's the kind of hook that only comes about one way. I had an overwhelming suspicion that the hook for *Thirteen* must have come long before Steve ever put pen to paper on it, so I asked him. And yes — the concept and the hook came first, and the book was written around it in exactly the same way as I did with *Her Last Tomorrow* and *Tell Me I'm Wrong*.

The hook for *Thirteen* is the ultimate lesson in leading the reader down a path then turning around and smacking them in the face with a shovel. It also tells us something else, albeit in a less direct way: it ups the **stakes**. If the serial killer is on the jury, we don't need anyone to tell us what the stakes are there. Likewise with *Tell Me I'm Wrong*, the fact that Megan discovers something which makes her suspect her husband is a serial killer is enough to get the stakes across. You don't need me to add *AND SHE MIGHT DIE* on the end. That'd be like using a sledgehammer to crack a nut.

*Her Last Tomorrow's* stakes are far more explicit. The hook is all about the stakes. If he doesn't murder his wife, he doesn't save his daughter. That's why that hook was so successful — it was a question with personal pronouns, an impossible choice and high stakes. You could even argue it was a what-if, only worded differently. It had almost a full house of hookiness.

There are many things that can make a hook hooky, but I find they're the six things that can make your tagline sing. Let's look at them again.

- **Questions**
- **Personal pronouns**
- **Impossible choices**
- **What ifs**
- **Twists of logic**
- **Stakes**

You'll notice I made a mention of **markers of genre** earlier, but didn't include it in the list. Although making the genre clear is very helpful, if not essential, it's not going to make the hook any hookier, so it doesn't count as an active ingredient any more than 'write it in the language your audience speaks' or 'use actual letters instead of runes' would. But it is something that'd be rather helpful in enabling your potential readers to understand what's going on.

So if you write a hook that has a question, a personal pronoun, and a what if, you'll sell thousands of books, right? Not quite. There are a couple of other things you need to consider.

First of all, you have to **make it original**. You might think the biggest possible stakes (particularly in a sci-fi or action thriller book) are that the world will end.

You're wrong. That's been done to death so many times, literally no-one gives a shit anymore.

Every Bond film has the same stakes (and yes, it works for them, but that's because it's what the audience *expects*). So aliens are threatening to blow up the planet. So what? Not only is it unoriginal, but it's not **something we can relate to**. It's so far-fetched, it doesn't count as having anything realistic at stake.

What might seem less dramatic and action-packed can actually be far *more* dramatic in the story-telling sense, as it will allow the reader (or potential reader) to connect with it and think *Wow, that could be me*.

What it all boils down to is this: you need to **make us care**. And I mean really care. That doesn't mean making it overly dramatic. It means singing to the core of human instincts. Open up those animalistic fears. Stand apart from the crowd and give us no option but to buy that book to see what happens.

# WHAT MAKES A GOOD HOOK?

One of the comments I most commonly get from students on my *Writing Killer Blurbs and Hooks* course (don't forget your 40% discount!) is that hooks only seem to be used effectively for psychological thrillers.

This is wrong.

Each of my successes with hooks has been with psychological thrillers, so of course that's what I know best. But powerful, high-concept hooks can be used in *all* genres and there are a number of remarkable patterns I've identified which could enable you to write the next killer hook.

Let's have a look at a few.

Five students go to detention. Only four leave alive.

ONE OF US IS LYING — KAREN M.
MCMANUS (YOUNG ADULT FICTION)

The serial killer isn't on trial. He's on the jury.

THIRTEEN — STEVE CAVANAGH
(THRILLER)

This is the way the world ends. For the last time.

FIFTH SEASON — N.K. JEMSIN
(DYSTOPIAN)

They're not the heroes we deserve. They're just the
ones we could find.

AURORA RISING — KAY KRISTOFF
AND AMIE KAUFMAN (SCIENCE
FICTION)

There are some clear patterns emerging as we look at
those examples, and they all exploit an extremely
powerful psychological quirk.

Notice how they each have two sentences. The first
sentence is always pretty mundane and ordinary. *Five*

*students go to detention. The serial killer isn't on trial. This is the way the world ends. They're not the heroes we deserve.* This is the setup.

Next, in the second sentence, the whole premise is turned on its head in one way or another. In ONE OF US IS LYING, we discover one of the students is going to die.

Five students go to detention. Only four leave alive.

ONE OF US IS LYING — KAREN M.<br>MCMANUS (YOUNG ADULT FICTION)

In Steve Cavanagh's book, the opening premise that the serial killer isn't on trial isn't massively surprising. So they got the wrong guy. Whoop-de-doo. But wait. What's that?

The serial killer isn't on trial. He's on the jury.

THIRTEEN — STEVE CAVANAGH<br>(THRILLER)

Holy shit, there's your hook. The guy's sitting there on the jury, literally deciding the fate of the person being charged for his crimes.

In the hook for FIFTH SEASON, not only is the world ending (surprising for dystopian fiction, no?) but this time it's *actually* ending.

> This is the way the world ends. For the last time.
>
> FIFTH SEASON — N.K. JEMSIN
> (DYSTOPIAN)

My early morning brain is struggling to cope with the concept of dystopian fiction in which there *is* no after, but I think this is what makes it such a powerful hook for readers of the genre in the same way putting the serial killer on the jury would catch the breath of crime and thriller fans.

The hook for AURORA RISING is a little less direct and a little less stunning, but nonetheless it follows the format and provides a whimsical, quirky atmosphere which accompanies much science fiction in some form or another.

> They're not the heroes we deserve. They're just the ones we could find.
>
> AURORA RISING — KAY KRISTOFF AND
> AMIE KAUFMAN (SCIENCE FICTION)

This pattern is nothing new. And it wasn't invented by authors or publishers' marketing teams, either. Have a little look at these one-liner jokes and see if you can spot any familiar patterns:

Crime in multi-storey car parks. That is wrong on so many different levels.

TIM VINE

When I was younger I felt like a man trapped inside a woman's body. Then I was born.

YIANNI

Life is like a box of chocolates. It doesn't last long if you're fat.

JOE LYCETT

My wife told me: 'Sex is better on holiday.' That wasn't a nice postcard to receive.

JOE BOR

The whole concept of a one-liner joke is to create a

perfectly normal and mundane setup, before pulling the rug from under their feet and completely turning it on its head. We're in the realm of puns, a lot of the time.

Our brains are wired to take these surprises and enjoy them. We like to be fooled, as long as the outcome is funnier or more satisfactory in some way than we were expecting. It's the reason why we try to guess the killer in a murder mystery but don't always like getting it right. It's why we like movies with huge twists at the end.

In Yianni's joke, the listener assumes Yianni is either a transgender man or has experienced some other type of gender dysmorphia. Then he drops the punchline and we realise he was talking about his own mother's pregnancy all along.

> When I was younger I felt like a man trapped inside a woman's body. Then I was born.
>
> YIANNI

Joe Lycett's joke has a similar style to the hook for AURORA RISING (*They're not the heroes we deserve. They're just the ones we could find.*) in that its setup is an already familiar and well-known turn of phrase. We think we know what's coming next. But we're wrong.

Again, we've been fooled. But the writer has delivered something even more satisfactory in the form of humour.

Life is like a box of chocolates. It doesn't last long if you're fat.

JOE LYCETT

In Joe Bor's joke, we're led to believe he's been having a discussion with his wife about her preferring sex on holiday. Then, boom. The punchline reveals she's been having sex on holiday without him.

My wife told me: 'Sex is better on holiday.' That wasn't a nice postcard to receive.

JOE BOR

Cue stunned hilarity.

Of course, not all hooks have to be formed in this exact way, but creating a setup and then throwing in a huge twist is an extremely powerful tool. It permeates all areas of our psychology. It's the basis for our sense of humour and the dominant flavour in all our best-loved movies. It appeals to a far deeper part of the human brain. It stands out.

And if you can do it in as few words as the examples in this chapter, you're onto a winner.

# TAKING A LOOK AT THE SILVER SCREEN

I've mentioned hooks in the same sentence as high-concept ideas and elevator pitches before, and it's fair to say that there are a number of different interconnected dramatic devices which have more or less the same effect.

As always, it's about catching attention quickly and effectively.

Hollywood has perfected this art over many years, and some movies have managed to nail the hook perfectly.

With movies, there's no really obvious pattern or formula in the same way we tend to see in one-liner jokes or book hooks — but the concept is the same. Use as few words as possible to shock and surprise, stand out and hook people into *having* to find out more.

Let's have a look at a few examples.

They're young... they're in love... and they kill people.

BONNIE & CLYDE

Whoever wins, we lose.

ALIEN VS. PREDATOR

Earth. It was fun while it lasted.

ARMAGEDDON

Her life was in their hands. Now her toe is in the mail.

THE BIG LEBOWSKI

At least three out of four of those movie taglines follow a similar sort of pattern to the one-liner jokes and novel hooks we looked at in the last chapter.

# HOW TO AVOID WRITING A BAD HOOK

In the last chapter, I touched on what *not* to do with regard to action thrillers and sci-fi (you remember: the 'end of the world' stuff). I didn't want to go too far into it and dilute the message of that chapter, so I think it merits its own special place in the book.

Every genre will have its tropes — things readers expect. That's all well and good, and yes — your romance novel *should* have two lovers who are kept apart by external forces and eventually get together. Yes, your crime book absolutely should have a despicable and seemingly unsolvable crime which the detective manages to crack at the last minute. Of course they should. That's what *makes* it a romance or a crime novel. That's what genre *is*.

Read that again. That's what <u>genre</u> is. It's not what your hook is. Your hook is what makes your book stand apart from the others; not what throws it into the same pool as them.

The following, whilst they might sound great, will not suck in readers like whacking great electromagnets:

## Crime

*A killer is on the loose. Can Detective Johnson catch him before it's too late?*

Well, yes. He can. In fact, he must. Otherwise it wouldn't be a crime book.

## Romance

*He's a corporate millionaire. She's his personal assistant. Can they find true love?*

I'd imagine so, after a few hundred pages of coy glances and bending each other over his desk.

. . .

## Sci-fi

*The intergalactic war has raged for five thousand years. Now Earth itself is at risk.*

Of course it is. I'd expect nothing else from a military space opera. It sounds great. But it's not going to hook people in.

## Historical fiction

*With the Russian Empire on the brink of collapse, can Admiral Vasily Naborkov avoid catastrophe?*

No. Although I invented Admiral Naborkov three seconds ago, I know enough about the Crimean War to know it wasn't Russia's finest hour. Nor do I give a damn about whether any catastrophes were avoided. Why? For the same reason I don't care about any of those 'hooks': they're dry. They're unoriginal. Although they use lots of dramatic words, the fact is they're *boring*.

Apologies to anyone whose taglines or blurbs are even vaguely similar to any of those. I promise, I quite literally just spewed them out inside less than ten seconds each. If by some coincidence they happen to sound like one of your taglines, you should take it as a sign you're *definitely* doing it wrong.

# HOW TO FIND THE HOOK IN
# YOUR BOOK

I'm about to either upset you or reassure you. But please, bear with me.

Not every book can have a killer hook.

Still here? Good. Now let me explain.

There's a lot to be said for writing a book around its hook, rather than the other way round. That's not to say it can't be done retrospectively — far from it — but the eagle-eyed amongst you might have noticed that I have over twenty books published and only two of them (at the time of writing) have killer hooks that have allowed me to make some serious money out of them.

Yes, not even *I* can find a killer hook in a rather average run-of-the-mill book, which the vast majority of mine are. But there are two things I a) fervently believe, b) have tested and c) you can apply to your own books.

1. You can write a hook or tagline for each one of your books and increase the sales of all of them.

2. You can write a killer hook, build a storyline around it and end up with a golden egg in marketing terms.

I'm not going to lie to you. If you're trying to write a hook for a book you've already written, you're fighting an uphill battle. That's not to say it's impossible, but it is a lot more difficult than coming up with a killer hook and then writing the book around it.

Out of my twenty or so books, maybe three of them have what I'd consider to be marketable hooks. By 'marketable hooks', I mean a distilled phrase of fewer than ten words which I can use on its own in a marketing campaign to draw huge amounts of attention to the book.

Sure, I can distil every single one of my books down into a tagline of fewer than ten words. Some of them are even good. But my standards for a *marketable* hook are high.

So, I've got you on the floor. I've told you writing hooks is hard, told you most of your own hooks are rubbish and that you've got next to no chance of writing a decent hook for *any* of your existing books. Time to give up, right?

Wrong.

Although you're unlikely to come up with a *Could*

*you murder your wife to save your daughter?* or *The serial killer's not on trial. He's on the jury* for an existing book that isn't built around one of these high concepts, if you apply my techniques to your existing hooks and taglines properly, *you will very likely boost your sales.*

For the sake of a couple of hours spent developing what already exists, you can easily boost your conversion rates and — essentially — pick up free money. Besides which, it'll be great practice for finding what works, ready to start developing those unique killer hooks which will spark your next great novel.

So, you've already got a book or a number of books. Great. How do you find the hooks?

## 1. Get out of your own head.

You know the story. You wrote it. You know how it ends. You know how it *feels.* And the problem with that is you're too close to it. You can't see what a potential reader browsing Amazon sees when they come across your book.

When you look at your product page, you see the title and think 'Cor, I'm dead chuffed with that title. It fits in really well with what happens in chapter 36.' You see the cover and wonder if perhaps you should've gone with the one the red overlay on the title. It's all irrelevant. The potential reader knows nothing of any of this. They're seeing it for the first time with fresh eyes. Everything you considered and thought about is invisible.

It will be almost impossible for you to shake those existing preconceptions about your own book, but you have to try. If you're using your new hook for your ongoing marketing campaigns, and putting it front and centre (as you should), it'll be the first thing they see. First impressions count. Look at the examples I've used time and time again in this book. See how they make an instant impact and leave you breathless, wanting more.

*Could you murder your wife to save your daughter?*

*The serial killer's not on trial. He's on the jury.*

If you're browsing through Facebook and you see one of those sentences alongside an eye-catching image, there's no way you're scrolling past it.

## 2. Work out the beats

If you're a plotter, you'll probably already have a beat sheet or an approximation thereof. If you're a pantser, it's time to make one.

Plot out your story's main beats, ignoring all the stuff

that doesn't drive the central plot. You should have no more than a dozen beats at most, for the purposes of this exercise. It'll give you a basic skeletal overview of your story, which you can use to distance yourself from it.

What is the question you're asking of the reader? Is there an impossible choice to be made? What are the twists that'll take our breath away? What are the stakes for the main characters? How do those stakes relate to our primal fears?

### 3. Make us care

The truth is, we don't care about your character. We've never heard of him or her. Assume we've never heard of you, either. Why do I want to take time out of my day and money out of my bank account to buy your book and see what happens? I'm sure it's a good book. I reckon it's great. But there are lots of great books out there and *OH MY GOD THAT ONE HAS SUCH A GOOD HOOK I'M BUYING THAT ONE.* Bye bye. One more lost sale.

I don't know you. I don't know your books. I don't know your world. How is your book relevant to *me* and *my world*? How does it play on my own fears and instincts? Don't just speak to the reader; speak to their primal selves.

Listing out the beats in your story had its purpose in helping you distance yourself and try to extract any twists, impossible choices and stakes. Now you've done that, forget the plot. We're going primal.

We need to look at what fears drive all humans.

# PART 3

# UNDERSTANDING THE PSYCHOLOGY

# USING WHAT DRIVES US

We are all driven by primal fears and instincts. Evolutionary biologists estimate there are five primal fears which all humans share. This might seem like I'm going off-topic, but bear with me. All hooks have their basis in one of the five primal human fears, so understanding what they are is crucial to developing your own killer blurbs and hooks.

**1. Extinction.** Woah, hold your horses for a moment, sci-fiers. We're not talking 'end of the world' stuff here. This is also the fear of personal extinction. The fear of death. The sense that you might not be here any more, that the world will carry on without you. It's the fear of no longer being.

. . .

**2. Mutilation.** This is the fear of your body being invaded or parts of it being taken from you. It's believed most fears of bugs or animals are driven by this, and it's also the basis for many people's fear of developing a neurological disorder or dementia.

**3. Loss of autonomy.** This drives many other health worries, as well as the ones mentioned above. It also feeds into claustrophobia and can drive commitment phobias. It's all to do with a fear of losing control, no longer having your own independence. Your reaction to kidnapping or imprisonment would be largely driven by this primal fear.

**4. Separation.** This is one of the earliest primal fears we develop in childhood. Anyone who's had children knows that all babies go through a stage of severe separation anxiety.

My own son wouldn't let either of us leave the room for a good few weeks. He'd cry if we put him down. His brain had got to the point where he understood who we were and was starting to develop a love for us and a bond with us. He knew he *needed* us to survive. He couldn't feed himself. He also understood we could disappear and go into other rooms, but he wasn't yet able to crawl or walk to come with us. For all he knew, we were never coming back.

Although we all grow out of that particular type of separation anxiety (and, thank goodness, so has my son) it manifests itself in different ways in adulthood. We fear our loved ones dying or leaving us, we fear rejection, we fear not being wanted or valued by other people. Anyone who's ever received the silent treatment will understand this fear of separation or rejection.

**5. Ego-death.** This is a little harder to explain, but in essence it's the fear of being humiliated or shamed. Anything that feeds into the loss of integrity of the self is a form of ego-death. We all construct our own worlds and outlooks on life. To have those shattered can be devastating.

So, how do those primal fears feed into hooks and blurbs for books? Let's take a look at some of the examples we've used numerous times already, and see how they play on our primal fears.

*Could you murder your wife to save your daughter?*

The fear of **separation** is strong on this one. To never see your child again is one of the most devastating fears a parent can have. This hook also hints at a loss of **autonomy** (Nick has no control over his own life or destiny: he must murder his wife or his daughter dies) and, like all good psychological thrillers, has a strong element of **ego-death**. Nick's world is turned upside down in an instant and everything he believed to be true and constant is no longer either of those things.

*What if you discovered your husband was a serial killer?*

**Ego-death** is perhaps the strongest player here. That sentence turns your world upside down immediately. Your loved one, your husband, the person you trust and depend on the most, is revealed to be one of the most despicable humans alive. The fear of **extinction** is quite an obvious one too, if you're living in the same house as a serial killer.

·   ·   ·

*The serial killer's not on trial. He's on the jury.*

Again, **ego-death** takes over here. The known and accepted truths (that killers sit in the dock and impartial members of the public are on the jury) is turned on its head and nothing is true anymore. There are obvious fears of **extinction** and, to an extent (and leading up to the extinction) quite a high chance of **mutilation**. This hook, however, is less about the stakes (which are undeniably high) and more about the uniqueness of the concept and the thought of 'How the *hell* did that happen, and how is it going to play out?'

All of our fears, betrayals, confusions and horrors are driven in some way by these five primal fears. They're the bases for everything else, so knowing them will enable you to build up from there as well as identifying the real primal fears you need to tap into, either in finding the hook in your existing book or developing your next hook and plot.

There are plenty of other things that need to be borne in mind, though.

It might be tempting to think that the fear of death (**extinction**) is the most dramatic and marketable fear to build a hook around. Not only has it been done to death (ho ho ho) but it's so dramatic it's almost cliché.

Remember: most readers are female, and most of the people who respond to adverts are female. Appealing to a female mind is likely to yield higher rewards than trying to appease our simple male brains.

Although we all share the same primal fears, the exact dosages do vary. Hooks and taglines which trigger primal fears in females are more likely to be about **separation** and **ego-death**.

End-of-the-world thrillers and high-octane, gun-driven books which play on the fears of **extinction** and **mutilation** tend not to sell so well with female audiences. That's not to say women don't read action thrillers, of course, but we're talking about playing the odds here.

That's why psychological thrillers have become such huge business in the last few years. They usually have domestic settings and play on the primal fears and instincts to which the female mind is most suited. They don't involve spies or aliens or vampires — these are real fears, real people, real scenarios that could happen to anyone, and that's where the fear factor hits home.

That's also why I believe hooks are easier to write for psychological thrillers than most other genres. It's the genre which plays most heavily on our primal fears; it's the genre which is defined by its ability and compulsion to do so. It's a genre which is very difficult to get right, but which speaks to all of us when done properly.

But by building those primal fears into hooks for your own particular genre, you can cross that threshold of speaking personally to the reader (or potential reader) and investing them in what happens. That is how you make them care — by speaking to their primal instincts and giving them no option but to be magnetised to your book.

Killer blurbs and hooks can be written for books of all genres. We've already looked at plenty of examples throughout this book. And the reason they tend to be easier and more natural for psychological thrillers? Because that taps into the root of what makes us tick.

And this is where things get even more interesting. We've taken a look at the primal fears which drive all (or most) humans. Which of those apply to your story?

How can you maximise the effect of your hook or blurb by using pure psychology? How can you make people *need* to buy your book?

That's what we're going to have a look at now.

# PERSUASION

We spend our entire existence being persuaded to do things, whether we like it or not. Our lives are filled with adverts, constantly trying to influence and cajole us into doing things, but rarely ever actually *telling* us to do them.

This is where the psychology of persuasion comes in.

The long-touted wisdom when it comes to book blurbs (and, indeed, any kind of splash or landing page on the internet) has been to go in for the hard sell, then close with a strong call to action (Buy this great product today!).

That's weird, because it's been known since long before the days of the internet that this is *not* the best way to get people to do things.

Influence has a number of different triggers, and some of them can be extremely powerful. 'Hey, you, do this!' tends not to be one of them. Sure, it can work — and it often does — but there are far more powerful tools at your disposal if you take a little time to learn about them and how to use them.

The human mind is simple. We often overthink things, but we don't need to. The brain is infinitely hackable, and hacking brains is what sales and marketing pros have been doing for years, in a non-abbatoiry kind of way.

At this stage, I'd recommend getting yourself a copy of Robert B. Cialdini's book *Influence: The Psychology of Persuasion*. It's the go-to book for this sort of stuff, although I'm going to summarise and explain some of the most pertinent bits I learned from the book here.

In the book, Cialdini references a number of psychological experiments with some intriguing and exciting results.

One of them focuses around just one word.

## Because

It's an innocuous word. It precedes extra information or an explanation of some sort. It's also the complete, unabridged answer you get when you ask a teenager

'Why?'. But, that aside, it's also one of the most powerful psychological tools in your persuasive arsenal.

In the catchily named 1978 study, *The Mindlessness of Ostensibly Thoughtful Action: The Role of "Placebic" Information in Interpersonal Interaction*, Ellen Langer, Arthur Blank and Benzion Chanowitz asked people to do things. And no, that's not me being vague.

The results of their study were mind-blowing.

They joined a queue at a photocopier and tried pushing in. Those already in the queue seemed to be compliant in general, but it's the detail that matters.

When they asked someone 'Excuse me, I have five pages. May I use the machine?' 60% of people let them do so.

When the question was tweaked to 'Excuse me, I have five pages. May I use the machine because I'm in a rush?' compliance rose to an incredible 94%.

So was the difference due to the fact they were in a rush? They tested this, and asked another question (not to the same people, because that would be stupid). This time, they asked 'Excuse me, I have five pages. May I use the machine because I have to make some copies?' Compliance was 93% — almost identical to them asking because they were in a rush.

The results were staggering. Simply adding a reason, preceded by 'because' made compliance rates skyrocket.

And the reasons weren't all that compelling, either. After all, who isn't in a rush? And of course he wanted to use the machine because he had to make some copies — he was queueing for a bloody photocopier! It doesn't matter how BS the reason is — just adding 'because' can make all the difference.

## The 6 Principles of Persuasion

In Cialdini's book, he highlights the six 'weapons of influence' which can be used to bring about a change of behaviour in others, each based on a psychological principle of persuasion.

Some of them may not be relevant to your life as an author and publisher, but they're well worth familiarising yourself with. You never know when they might come in useful. They are:

### Reciprocity
When we are given something, we feel an obligation to do something in exchange. Free books in exchange for a newsletter signup, perhaps?

### Consistency
We feel compelled to act according to our past expe-

riences and actions, and to be consistent in what we do. Changing our views and actions is uncomfortable.

## Social proof

If we come across something new or are unsure as to what action to take, we look to others. Has this book sold a million copies already? Wow. It must be good. I'd better buy it.

## Liking

If we already like the person asking us to do something, we're far more likely to do it. This is why building a relationship with your readers is so vital.

## Authority

As humans, we tend to obey figures of authority or perceived authority, as well as people with titles or greater levels of expertise.

## Scarcity

We see things as being more valuable if they are less available. Limited time offers force people to act now.

When it comes down to it, we humans are pretty

simple beings. We're all driven by a series of straightforward innate impulses and desires.

Indeed, this is what makes any story appeal to us so much. That's why stories need to have a particular structure and end in a satisfying manner. It's not about being original, but about satisfying that primal need which has been in all humans since the dawn of time and which will – probably — always be there.

And that's why the principles of marketing and advertising never change, either. Sure, there might be a new dashboard or bidding system to learn. Certain visual styles or colour schemes might be more prevalent at different times to others. But the basic, underlying psychology and the innate drivers of what actually resonates with people has never changed and will never change.

# THE PSYCHOLOGY OF PRICING

## Double or nothing?

In Robert Cialdini's book (which is the bible when it comes to this stuff. Buy it) he talks of a jewellery store which was struggling to shift some remaining stock.

They kept dropping the prices, but the stock wouldn't shift. A passer-by mentioned they might want to try *raising* the prices. This, of course, was madness. Right? Right?

The jewellery store owner *doubled* the original retail price of the stock. It sold almost immediately.

Why is this?

To put it in its most simple form, it's a case of psychological shortcutting and perception.

We are exposed to too many external environmental

stimuli each day to be able to process everything that comes in. As a result, the human brain deploys a complexity reduction system almost constantly throughout your everyday life.

It's precisely why we *do* judge a book by its cover. It's why we *do* look at people and make a snap judgement about them. We don't have the time to learn the life story, personality traits and motivations of every single person we come across. If we see a guy with a shaved head, tattoos and a growling dog, we assume he wants to nick our wallets and have our knackers for breakfast.

This complexity reduction system works by introducing shortcuts based on past experiences. It's exactly what makes phobias occur. If you had a traumatising incident with a fox, balloon or signed photo of Robert Mugabe when you were younger, you're likely to associate those items with negative feelings. And in at least two of those situations, you'd be right. I mean, who likes foxes or balloons?!

It's this complexity reduction system which sold that guy's jewellery. When he lowered the price, people perceived it as being an indicator of low quality. When he doubled the retail price, the quality of the product was perceived as being much higher, so the product itself was much more desirable.

If you browse any of the book club groups on Facebook, the subject of pricing comes up quite often. People tend to be split into a few camps. First is the 'I don't buy anything above 99p' camp. The second is the 'I don't buy anything under £4.99' camp. The third is the 'I'd give my first-born's kidneys for this author's next book' camp. The second and third are the ones you want, although I'd be wary about complicity in trafficking human body parts.

If you're courting readers who only buy 99p and permafree, you're going to need *millions* of them in order to make any money. And you won't be able to advertise with profit margins that small, either.

The readers you want are the ones who are happy to spend £4.99 (or donate their children's vital organs) for a book. They're the ones you want to court, so don't fall into the trap of trying to please the 99p crowd.

That said, discount days and BookBub Featured Deals are still well worth doing. Lots of readers use these sites not just to get cheap or free books, but to discover new authors and series. My point is that discounting and low pricing shouldn't be your primary strategy, and freebie seekers shouldn't be your prime audience.

## Why permafree sucks (and doesn't suck)

Don't worry, I'm not sitting on the fence here. I rarely sit on the fence with anything, and especially not with a bare backside.

Now, I'm straying a little distance away from the purpose of this book, but while we're on the subject of the psychology of persuasion and how the pricing strategy you employ affects that, it's worth me briefly dipping into the permafree quagmire. If nothing else, you'll get an insight into what I do, and what works for me.

Permafree itself has some distinct advantages and disadvantages. It allows you to find as many readers as possible, by taking the financial transaction out of the decision making process. Why wouldn't they take a punt? It costs them nothing. On the flip side of that, you're spending money to court readers who don't want to part with money for books. That's not a great business model for an author or publisher.

Readthrough from permafree is generally very low. Anyone with an ereader will know how easy it is to fill the device up with free books which never get read. Yours will be on thousands of devices in much the same way. And if you've paid for people to download that free book in the form of advertising and marketing, it's all pretty pointless.

That said, of course there *is* readthrough from permafree, and a large number of my readers discovered my books in exactly this way. But it's hard work, and the hit rate is a lot lower than people assume. A 2% readthrough from permafree to paid-for book two is not unreasonable. That's only one in fifty, but it's actually pretty good by industry standards.

But raise the price to 99p/99c and it suddenly skyrockets. Why? Cognitive dissonance.

Cognitive dissonance happens when your brain tries to make sense of two conflicting realities. It's exactly the reason why people fawn over £3,000 handbags. I mean, you wouldn't be so stupid as to spend £3,000 on an item you could get for £50, would you? No, of course not. So the £3,000 handbag *must* be of exceptional quality, despite all evidence to the contrary.

The same happens with books. If someone downloads a book for free, they've got no skin in the game. If they don't like it, it's because it was free. Value perception. Their brain didn't expect to like it.

But raise the price to just 99p/99c and people's attitudes change. They've placed a stake. They've invested. They don't want to feel as though they've been stupid and wasted their money, so they're likely to look on the book more favourably. That means they're more likely to read it, more likely to enjoy it and more likely to buy future books in the series.

Take a look at the reviews of permafrees and paid-for books and you'll see what I mean. The first books in each of my two series have been permafree for long periods of time over the past few years, and the reviews show it. When the books are paid-for, however, the reviews improve drastically.

Cognitive dissonance ensures our brains actually *change* our beliefs and feelings in order to justify our actions, in order to make us feel good about ourselves. And it's incredibly powerful.

This is why I cycle permafrees. The default position is to have my first-in-series books at 99p/£1.99 and fire some ads at it for a few months. Then I'll apply for a BookBub Featured Deal on it. If I'm successful, I'll make the book free for the period of the deal (and a little before and after, to do some promo stacking), top a few of the free book charts and ride the wave. Once that starts to dip down, I go back to paid-for and pick up that slow drip of readers who are likely to actually read through my series.

# PART 4
# LET'S GET PRACTICAL

# IT'S ALL IN THE WAY SHE LOOKS

I'm pretty sure that's a line from a song, but I've been writing for hours and if I dare Google it I know I'll get lost down a rabbit hole and find myself sitting here at three o'clock in the morning reading a Wikipedia article about Saudi Arabian goat herding practices.

Looks matter, though. I've seen some blurbs which are well written but look absolutely horrendous on a sales page. Formatting tools are your friend.

Let's have a look at a couple of examples.

Be the first to review this item

See all 2 formats and editions

| Kindle Edition | Paperback |
|---|---|
| £2.99 | £5.99 _prime_ |

Read with Our Free App | 1 New from £5.99

Westborough Central Courts. The Jury Find Her Not Guilty. She walks free from the Court. DCI Mandy Fleischman is in Shock at the Verdict. Five years later she returns as as 'Hannah' Who gets a Management Job at the Haulage Company. She begins her Killing Spree Again. DCI Mandy Fleischman is assigned to the Case. The Hunt is Now On For this Murderous Killer.

Apart from the fact that this is a pretty bloody awful blurb in almost every way, it also looks uninspiring. It's a big block of text which doesn't stand out in the slightest, other than to scream *FOR CHRIST'S SAKE PAY NO ATTENTION TO THIS BORING BIT*.

I could spend all day pulling that blurb to pieces, but for now let's just look at it aesthetically. Compare and contrast to this blurb:

'Gloriously dark, deliciously twisty' CLAIRE MACKINTOSH

**ONE FAMILY, TWO HOLIDAYS, ONE DEVASTATING SECRET**

To new nanny Amanda, the Temple family seem to have it all: the former actress, the famous professor, their three successful grown-up children. But like any family, beneath the smiles and hugs there lurks far darker emotions.

Sixteen years earlier, little Niamh Temple died while they were on holiday in Portugal. Now, as Amanda joins the family for a reunion at their seaside villa, she begins to suspect one of them might be hiding something terrible...

**And suspicion is a dangerous thing.**

That blurb makes good use of bold text to draw the eye towards certain parts, as well as clean paragraph formatting and spacing. It's not overdone, either. Gone are the days of 18pt bright orange headers and calls to action smashing people's faces in like literary breeze blocks.

It's neat, clean, lean and looks great. To do this, however, you'll need to enter your blurb as HTML code. Don't panic, though. It's a *lot* easier than you think.

## Making your blurb look good

When composing your blurb, I recommend using the free book description generator provided by Kindlepreneur. You can access it at https://kindlepreneur.com/amazon-book-description-generator.

It's very easy to use and allows you to format and display your blurb in any way you please. Go easy on the formatting, though. Try not to use different font sizes or go overboard. A little bit of bold text to highlight your hook or an important piece of text can go a long way.

Once you've done that, take the HTML code it produces and head over to Ablurb at https://ablurb.github.io. There, you can paste the code and double check that it all displays how you want it to. If it needs some tweaking, either head back to Kindlepreneur or edit the HTML code by hand (if you're totally new to HTML, that goes *way* beyond the scope of this book).

Once you're happy with how the blurb looks, you're ready to go.

Please note that not *all* retailers want your blurb in HTML form. Some do, some only take plain text and some take rich text. For the latter, you can simply paste the generated, formatted blurb output from Ablurb rather than the HTML code itself.

# PART 5
# OTHER STUFF

# SUMMARY

Considering how vital a proper blurb and hook can be to your book and your career, it's almost criminal that it's so easy to rewrite and change your blurb.

But anyone who's ever uploaded a book to KDP, Kobo, Apple or any of the other vendors knows how easy it is. And that's why I'm so passionate about getting hooks and blurbs right.

Please, for the love of God, don't go looking at my blurbs for inspiration. Don't assume I've done it right. I haven't. At the time of writing, revamping my blurbs and hooks has been on my long-term to-do list for over a year. I've done a few, but not many, as much of my time is now spent helping other authors and trying to keep up my own output of fiction.

As I've hinted at a few times during this book,

looking at what others are doing is never a particularly good idea. That's because most people are doing it wrong — even me.

We get lazy. Updating and changing blurbs across a number of platforms is difficult. We might even worry that changing our blurb will actually reduce sales of that book.

But we're indies. As long as you've saved the original version of your blurb somewhere, you can easily roll back if — for some reason — your new blurb fails to hit its mark. That'll give you some breathing space to start again and to try and write an even better blurb for that book.

I freely admit I don't know what will work in all genres. I don't know all genres intimately. I know what works in crime and certain veins of the thriller genre, and I've got a pretty good overview of what works in many others, but it doesn't matter too much.

As we've seen, the psychology behind story and what compels us to make a decision to purchase a book is common to all readers. And, let's face it, there's no such thing as 'a sci-fi reader' or 'a romance reader'. Most, if not all, of us read across a number of different genres according to our whim and fancy. Sure, there are tropes that we look for and recognise as part and parcel of a particular type of book, and these are great signposts for a reader as to what they're getting themselves into. But, at the same time, originality always stands out.

My approach is no doubt subtler than that of some other industry experts who specialise in blurb and hook writing. But, in a world where everyone on the internet is shouting 'buy this!', I believe that subtle psychology is the way to cut through that noise. And the science backs it up. Once you stop *telling* people to do things and make them *want* to do them, you've created a strong psychological pull — a pull which will almost always outperform any smack-in-the-face call to action. And it's a method which has not only stood the test of time over decades already, but which will continue to be true for many decades to come.

# THE INDIE AUTHOR MINDSET

There's a whole lot more to being an indie author than writing blurbs and hooks. As you'll no doubt have discovered by now, there's a huge number of things all authors need to do in order to give themselves a chance of success.

You'll have noticed from reading this book that my approach isn't based on get-rich-quick methods or trying to sell you the latest gold rush.

I focus only on proven, long-term, evergreen strategies which have always rung true and always will ring true. Nothing I ever advise will double your sales immediately or turn you into an overnight sensation. But each change you make will cause an incremental increase in your chances of success and your overall sales.

Together, each of those changes adds up quickly.

The result is bigger than the sum of its parts. And your success will be built on solid foundations. It won't be based on a short-term gold rush which could be over within a week, leaving you high and dry and floundering to find the next big thing and repeat it all again. Most of us don't discover a gold rush once. We sure as hell aren't going to manage it twice.

By focusing on the long-term, your solid foundations will ensure that you can weather most, if not all, storms. You'll have the tools at your disposal to adapt quickly and grow steadily.

That's the Indie Author Mindset in a nutshell. It's a school of thought which has been growing for some time, and which is based around the successful and flourishing Facebook group (which you can find at http://facebook.com/groups/IndieAuthorMindset/).

When I started writing and publishing, there was next to no advice available. The industry was brand new, and even those of us who were there at the start didn't know how it was going to play out.

Today, the truth is quite the opposite. There's too much information and advice out there, and most of it is next to useless. There are people who've sold a few thousand books offering themselves up as publishing gurus. Everyone's got an opinion, and everyone's opinion is right.

My aim is to cut through all of this and provide solid, evergreen advice for building a solid career — from someone who's been there and done it. No get-rich-quick promises, no gold rushes, no 'next big thing'. Just practical, sensible advice for doing things the right way.

It's about giving readers the best possible product and cutting no corners. It's about doing what the traditional wing of the industry can't do in terms of flexibility, responsiveness to change and direct reader interaction. It's about thinking long-term, way beyond the end of this year and even the next decade, making the book world better for everyone.

As indie authors, we're now in a position where we have a huge amount of control over the industry. Our ability to turn on a sixpence only enhances that. We need to use that responsibly and properly, and look beyond the ends of our noses. History will judge us.

If you want to learn more about indie publishing and increasing your book sales and fan base, my Indie Author Mindset courses are a great place to start. Don't forget, you're entitled to 40% off all my courses using the promo code EBOOK40. You can view all available courses at https://courses.indieauthormindset.com.

Each of the courses will have its own accompanying Indie Author Mindset Guide, just like this one, giving you an expanded and elaborated overview of the subject in hand, in a format which allows me to pass on even more information and background.

I hope you continue to enjoy these guides, as well as the courses, and I look forward to seeing you in the Indie Author Mindset Facebook group.

**Adam Croft**
**July 2019**

# WRITING KILLER BLURBS AND HOOKS

AN INDIE AUTHOR MINDSET GUIDE

ADAM CROFT